THIS COLORING BOOK BELONGS TO:

_____

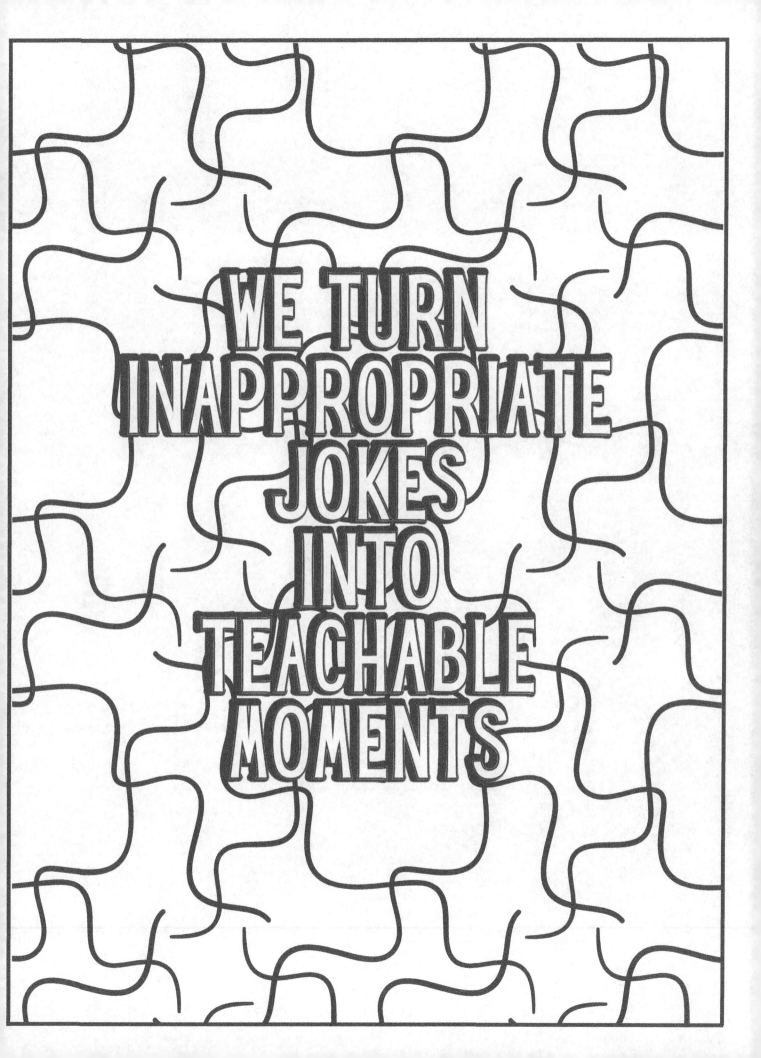

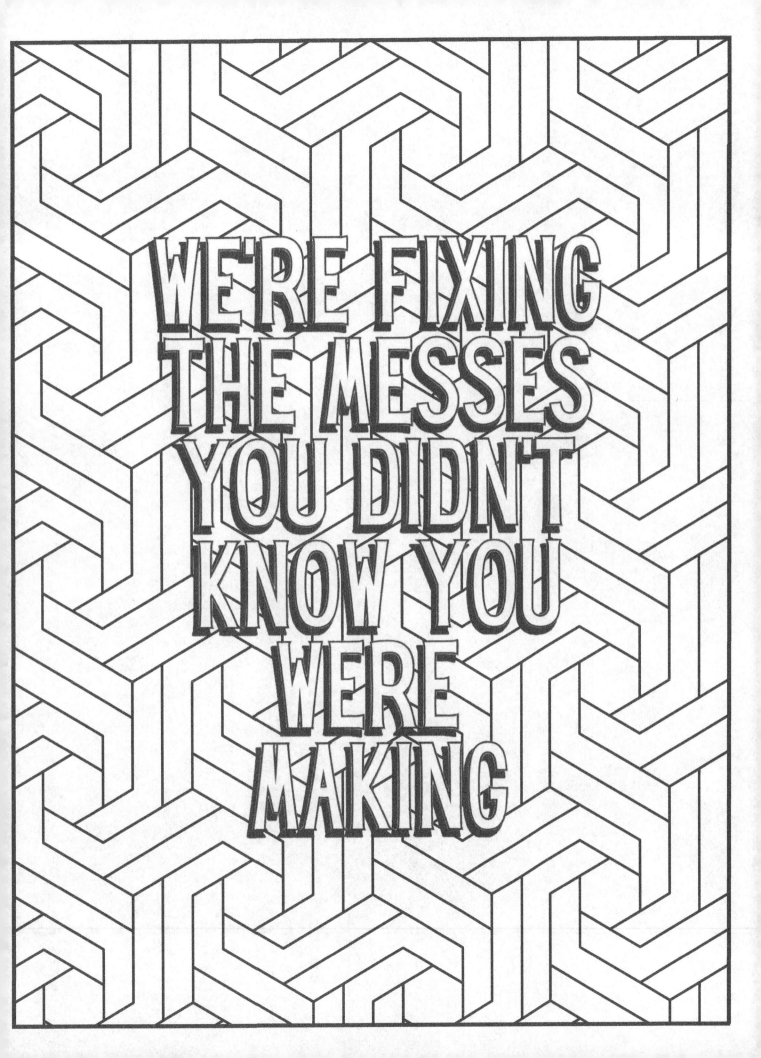

HR ADVICE: WHEN YOU FIND A BIG KETTLE OF CRAZY, IT'S BEST NOT TO STIR IT

HUMAN RESOURCES: BECAUSE DEALING WITH HUMANS IS NEVER A STRAIGHT LINE

HUMAN RESOURCES:
WHERE 'CAN I
SPEAK TO YOUR
MANAGER?' IS
OUR DAILY
ANTHEM.

HR EMERGENCY KIT:
A BOX OF TISSUES
A STACK OF FORMS
AND A SARCASM
FILTER

HR'S SUPERPOWER: KEEPING A STRAIGHT FACE DURING THE MOST RIDICULOUS REQUESTS

AS AN HR
PROFESSIONAL
I TAKE JUDGING
PEOPLE VERY
SERIOUSLY

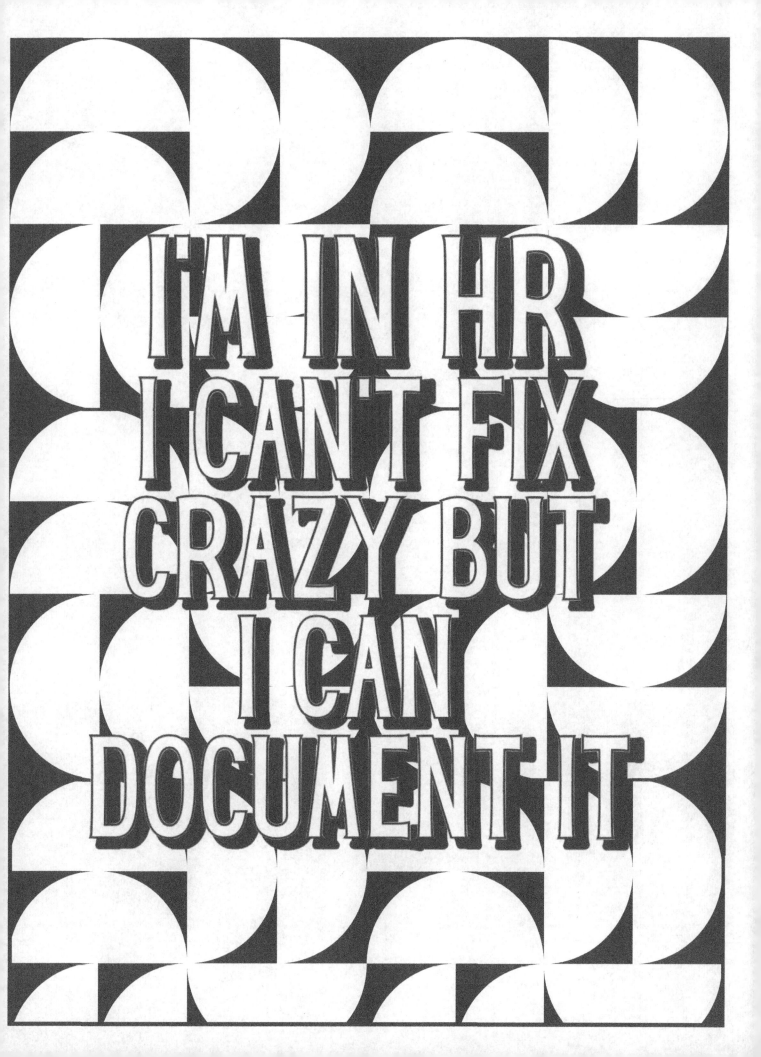

Made in the USA
Las Vegas, NV
12 December 2024

13950698R00046